Otherwhere

Acknowledgments

Thanks are due to the editors of the following publications, in which some of these poems, or versions of them, first appeared: *14 Magazine, City Lighthouse Poetry Anthology, New Writing South Poetry Anthology, New Writing Volume 15* (Granta/British Council), *Poetry London, Poetry Review, The Rialto, Trespass Magazine.*

'Look' was commended in the Torbay Open Poetry Competition, 2010. 'She Sits Like A Bird' was commissioned for Psycho-Poetica, a series of poems responding to Alfred Hitchcock's film Psycho, organised by Simon Barraclough.

Warm thanks to Ros Barber, Clare Best, Maureen Jivani, Kerrith Etkin-Bell, Sarah Salway, Jackie Wills, John Siddique, Tim Liardet, Liz Bahs, Monica Suswin, Alice Owens, Beth Miller, Fay Young, Neil Rollinson, Andie Lewenstein and Mark Ward for criticism, advice and umbrellas on rainy days.

I am very grateful to Arts Council England for a grant in 2009 which enabled me to commence work on this book; many thanks to Keiren Phelan, patron saint of bureaucracy-phobic poets.

For Nerissa, with love !

Otherwhere
Catherine Smith

Catherine
x

smith|doorstop

Published 2012 by
Smith/Doorstop Books
The Poetry Business
Bank Street Arts
32-40 Bank Street
Sheffield S1 2DS
www.poetrybusiness.co.uk

ISBN 978-1-906613-76-1

British Library Cataloguing-in-Publication Data.
A catalogue record for this book is available from the
British Library.

Typeset by Utter
Printed by Charlesworth
Cover design by Rob MacDonald

Smith/Doorstop Books is a member of Inpress,
www.inpressbooks.co.uk. Distributed by Central Books Ltd.,
99 Wallis Road, London E9 5LN.

Supported by
ARTS COUNCIL
ENGLAND

The Poetry Business is an Arts Council National
Portfolio Organisation

'What matters it how far we go?' his scaly friend replied.
'There is another shore, you know, upon the other side ....'

Lewis Carroll, *The Lobster-quadrille*.

'According to whether we are in the same place or separated
from each other, I know you twice. There are two of you.'

John Berger, *And Our Faces, My Heart, Brief as Photos*.

Contents

I.M. Greg Daville –
artist, friend and glorious work-in-progress.

Drought

Pavements shimmered, tarmac softened
and split; dog-shit powdered gutters.
In our garden, ochre grass needled
bare feet, compost heaps stank –
in dust-bowl flower-beds, begonias hung
parched, blowsy heads. Mum threw
dish-water on her Brother Cadfael roses;
grey liquid writhed through air, tiny moons
of fat clung to leaves. She had faith,
said we should pray for rain, but my head
was full of the rumour that had sparked,
crackled into life and spread like bush-fire
at lunch-break that day; if the heat continued,
pupils at the boys' school would be allowed
to sit exams in just their swimming trunks.
That night I twisted, sweating, dreamed
of the huge hall filling up with cold water,
blue ink bleeding into paper, of boys
kicking away chairs, the pool-echo
of their laughter; their slow, naked limbs
cleaving water. I woke to steady drumming
on the roof, raindrops splattering the patio,
the dying flowers redeemed and my body,
soaking; soaking, everywhere.

Blobs

I plug it in, sit back and watch
        the luminous orange wax swelling,
                rupturing, a sequence of bright blobs,

like eggs bursting from their follicles –
        look, a new creature, then another
                and another; I love the way they

gather momentum, bend their knees,
        spring, rise, rise ... now they're nuclear
                mushroom clouds wavering,

glowing planets, iridescent, detached
        placentas, headless Buddhas, dreaming
                Space Hoppers. Then I remember, or

think I remember, the dentist's whisper-
        quiet waiting room, and myself, seven,
                and a committed thumb-sucker,

enchanted by the ghost-fish tank
        standing on its own small table,
                laughing out loud at the blobs' blind,

innocent collisions, their buffoonery
        as they budged, jostled, kissed,
                the slow dramas they performed

for my amusement, these molten jellyfish.
        They make no sound but now, as then,
                I'm sure they're roaring in there, or

singing laments, or asking each other
        to dance. Over and over they burst,
                build, collapse, burst, build, collapse, like

this memory, where one moment I see
        my mother's face and hear
                the rustle of her magazine pages

and the next, everything blurs; I can't hear
        what she's whispering to me, or if she's
                whispering at all, as the blobs bump

against the surface: hesitate; fuse;
        everything they were has ended here,
                and like this memory, nothing moves.

Daughters

They're phantoms, nameless, but
they make their presence felt.

The one who sings *Summertime*
in the bathroom leaves taps running,

vanilla-scent lingering in the steam.
My earrings, tights, lipsticks vanish;

wine stains bloom on carpets.
5 a.m., there's one on the doorstep,

no key – sits with head in hands,
nauseous; vodka, I guess, flashbacks

to some boy's tongue in her mouth;
feet blistered, handbag spitting sequins.

She's dark, like me, but the fair ones
are like the dads they might have had –

the politics student from Leicester or
that Swedish physiotherapist on Kos.

Sometimes snatches of their laughter
seep downstairs – I imagine them

sprawled on the youngest one's bed,
painting each others' nails purple –

but often they squabble, their voices
raw and shrill as hungry crows.

When we all bleed on the same day,
the house shudders from banged doors.

In my mirror the singing one stands
behind me, combs her long wet hair –

meets my eyes for a few seconds,
then stares straight through me.

Blizzard

He's seven, hiding from his mother
in the airing cupboard, cross-legged
on the slats, breathing in the biscuity
scent of clean towels and ironed cotton;
he digs his thumb-nail into the ceiling's
loose plaster, peeling strips; it flutters,
slow and silent, his very own weather,
a private chalky blizzard –
the figure in a snow globe, up-ended,
shaken, he loves it here, this dark warmth,
thinks he might stay put all weekend,
but from the landing his mother's calling
Where are you? Where are you now?

Fall

The white-hot stinging cools,
gravel spits itself from palms,

knees, shins, blood funnels
back into veins, skin knits,

the trap-door of your mouth
crashes shut and the roar

leaps back into your throat.
You shoot up, backwards,

now you're sitting on the plank,
fingers curled around chains,

your knees unbend and you're up
in the juddering summer sky,

houses rising and falling –
Watch me, watch me, watch –

Fireflies

Because she hardly slept, and talked
too much, and asked too many questions,
they took her to a Psychiatrist, who said
she needed expert help, so they sent her
to school in the country, where the teachers
knew how to keep children calm and quiet,
and where questions were only allowed
at certain times and on certain subjects,
and mealtimes were silent because silence
is not only golden but good for the growing
brain – which was, they said, easily over-
stimulated by too much chatter and because
she couldn't stop the questions bubbling,
they sent her to bed at seven, and there
all the questions that couldn't be let out
flew from her mouth and through an open
top window and into the dusk, where they
glimmered like fireflies and danced all night.

Boys

Newborn boy, asleep, what
can you hear? – the tattoo
of a heart; slamming of blood?

Every cell in your body is a new
Universe, waiting
to blaze, then burn itself out.

And below us in the street,
five teenage boys
lurch home from clubbing,

bellowing into the night,
electric with lager and lust.
Once, they lay like you,

chests rising then falling
like collapsing loaves,
son; each one's finger

gripping a mother's finger
in his sleep, in his teeming,
astonishing sleep.

Helium

The teenage girls
with ironed hair

and perfect make-up
tug down sky-blue balloons

bumping the grey
of Caffè Nero's ceiling,

un-knot the necks,
suck down gas,

giggle questions
in Disney voices.

Then outside, to flirt
with builders, who

chuck and catch
scaffolding clamps –

each one clutched
with an *oof!*, each man

buckling with the weight.
We love you!

the girls squeak
and the men

love them back.
Keep laughing, girls,

rise up, go now,
before it's too late,

soar into the sky,
above the traffic,

schools, houses,
shops and offices,

the arms of anyone
who'd ever ground you.

Mussolini

A wet Wednesday lunchtime;
I'm fifteen, perched on the edge
of the teacher's desk,

and holding court
with my Miss Clavell impersonation –
crossing my legs,

imagining them
long and shapely
in shimmering American Tan.

I see myself in a short skirt,
winding a long strand
of her black hair

around a manicured fingernail.
I've captured her voice
perfectly, a low purr –

Now, girls, who can tell me
five salient points about Mussolini?
This is better

than being pretty,
getting straight A's
or even having divorced parents –

the girls are lapping me up,
their eyes gleaming
like night foxes.

And then the silence
which I miss by three seconds –
so I'm still mid-flow

when I see her in the doorway,
one hand on her hip –
she could so easily crush me

under one polished shoe –
she could grind me to dust,
so there'd be no trace –

and our eyes lock,
I try to uncross my legs
and can't.

Sister

Hauled out sixteen years ago today,
chests glued, facing each other

like lovers; never a moment
apart. Or a meal, a bath, a shit.

You're great at Maths, remember
birthdays, never leave wet towels

or knickers on the bathroom floor;
have perfect pitch, speak three

languages, praise God in all
of them. Our parents love you best.

I watch you sleeping and will your heart
to stutter to a standstill, think of you

sliced from me: the clear, light space.

Bonny

When I bump into Dennis he hugs me
and says, in his delicious Geordie accent,
My, but you're looking bonny!

Back home, I consult the dictionary.
Bonny: adj: comely, pretty; plump.
Suddenly it's clear: inside me

there's a Nineteenth Century
north-country farm girl,
reared on porridge, stew and dumplings,

rounded cheeks ruddy from
knifing sea-winds,
breasts pillowing over her blouse;

and every red-blooded local lad
can't wait to lure her into a fusty hay-loft,
press her down, lift her woolen skirt,

part her generous thighs to suckle
sweet folds of swollen flesh. At this moment
of promise, life's rude, dangerous;

I'll have to hide her well, this bonny girl –
button her tight inside my skin,
cut down on meat and dairy –

check for wisps of straw before
I venture out; make sure her laughter
doesn't bubble up through me.

The Lost Cats

Standing in Arrivals, you're becoming increasingly anxious
      about your luggage. It's been a long, gruelling tour,
most of the band are in the Gents snorting coke with the Tech guys.
      The carousel slumps around, piled with
the lead singer's five Burberry matching cases, you drag them off,
      where the hell is your bag, you need to know –
you'd recognise its battered green leather anywhere, the family crest,
      two crossed machetes – there's still no sign –
which is *terrible* because this morning you packed the cats in it –
      nested them among your soiled evening dress
and sweat-grimed boiler suit, they haven't been fed
      since Reykjavik. They're barely more than kittens,
tortoiseshell, with milky blue eyes, semi-feral. You won them in a poker game
      and feel responsible. Maybe the bag wasn't loaded,
maybe it's heading for Dalaman, perhaps some kindly baggage handler
      liberated them and is in the process of reporting the incident,
or maybe they've escaped and, somewhere in the bowels
      of the airport, they're already mating urgently,
among dust-balls and heating ducts. Before we know it Gatwick will be over-
      run with cats, curled asleep in waiting areas, rubbing
against the legs of cabin crew, running amok on runways. This is freaking you
      out. You flail your arms, shout, attract the attention
of a tall man in uniform, little gold wings on his jacket. *My bag's gone*
      missing, you tell him, *and the thing is –*
He shakes his head and produces a pale blue form. *Oh, don't tell me,*
      he says wearily, handing you a gold-tipped
fountain pen, *Cats, right? Yes,* you admit, ashamed. *Cats.*

Sparrows

My cat bites a sparrow's neck,
                drops it on the cream wool rug;
chomps contentedly through
                its grape-dark heart and pink lungs.
He leaves its neat head – both
                oil-black eyes; two tail feathers,
a bright red smear, then pads away.
                As I stand at the sink, scrubbing
bloodstains, I tell myself he's just
                obeying instincts – a sparrow
is prey to him; he cannot know
                in ancient China it was linked
to the penis, sometimes eaten
                for its potency, or in Greek myth,
an attribute of Aphrodite; or that
                in Western Art, a woman
holding a sparrow is a wanton.
                But as the water pinks, my eyes
sting with tears, because
                this creature was beautiful
and innocent and now it is dead.
                I think of Lesbia's pet sparrow,
limp in her lap; how she wept
                and wept until her eyes were raw.

Look

Here is the quiet child, always first
in the classroom, socks puddling

her ankles, kneeling like a supplicant
in the bright glow from the incubator

where day-old chicks have pecked
free from their shells and huddle

together in the sawdust, cheep-
cheeping their bewildered chorus.

See their yellow, curling feathers,
wobbling heads. The quiet child

takes a deep breath as she
lifts the lid, scoops one up,

it trembles in her hands, its beak
as soft as a baby's fingernail,

tapping the inside of her wrist
and the feeling is delicious,

a light tickling on the blue veins.
Look, here comes the teacher,

clapping her hands for registration
and the quiet child flinches,

squeezes her palms together
as if in prayer, and the chick's

tiny bones click quietly, like
the press-studs on her raincoat,

its galloping heart stutters, stops,
it's perfectly still now and look,

look, the quiet child slips it back
under the others and they hop

over it as though they don't know
what it is, the quiet child wipes

her nose on her cardigan sleeve,
slides into her seat, keeps her eyes

down as she says, *Here, Miss,*
and now she's sharpening her pencil,

curls of wood drifting like
black-edged feathers into her lap.

Silent Dining Room, St. Cuthman's

When I enter, just one Priest,
seated, with his back to me.
I put down my tray, quietly,
spoon fruit and plain yoghurt
into my mouth. The Priest
bites into his toast. I stare
at his long ears, flat against
his head, the thinning
hair – is he contemplating
God's goodness, or the tang
of the Roses' lime marmalade?
I try to concentrate on the silence –
how it blankets itself over
surfaces, wraps corners
of the mahogany furniture –
when, above the Priest's
gentle cough, my stomach
groans, then growls – now,
it's a furious Cerberus,
snarling at the entrance
to the underworld. I will it
to be silent; it won't behave,
gurgles like a bath emptying.
The Priest's back stiffens,
he stands, takes his tray,
pads past me on the polished
floorboards, his felt slippers
hardly registering a squeak.

Karma

On summer evenings,
I patrol my garden,
wrench every suctioned,
snot-trailing snail
from its stone or leaf,
hurl them over the fence,
punching the air as
each shell crunches
on my neighbour's patio.
I tell myself these snails
were once wife beaters,
dictators, paedophiles
or politicians. And that,
due to this insight,
in my next incarnation,
I'll be spared a life of
slow-motion shuffling
on one viscous foot,
a slave to chlorophyll.

The Poacher and the Hare

When I brought him home from the field, still warm,
and opened my cloak to show my wife what I'd done,
she gasped, turned her back on me, said she'd have
nothing to do with it, the trouble it would cause, but when
I laid him on the table, big fellow that he was, his long legs
curved like sickles, eyes clear as winter moons, she saw
he was handsome and noble and neither of us had put
so much as a mouthful of meat in our mouths for days –
she came to see the sense in it, so she sharpened her knife,
slit his belly all the way round, pulled his coat off over
his back legs, one neat tug, eased the fur over his head,
hacked off his little feet with his claws still grassy,
cut through the naked flesh and flopped the innards
into a bowl, and the blood was almost black
and full of goodness, and out came his heart and lungs
and wind-pipe – gentle, she was, reverent – she saved
the kidneys and liver and all the blood because
she never wasted any part of an animal, my wife,
even his feet she boiled up for soup, and I must say
he fried up a real treat and that was a supper
we savoured as though we were dining as grandly
as a Lord and Lady, oh he was a rare pleasure, that one.

*   *   *

But I tossed and turned that night, woke to moonlight
pouring like the sweetest mead through the window-hole,
I'd an itch to be out in the dark fields with the good earth
damp and rich under my feet but my wife pulled me back,
she was cold, she moaned, cold and numb to her poor bones
and I knew then how I should warm her so I lifted her arms,

pulled her smock over her head in one swift move
so she was naked and true as God made her, flipped her
over onto her belly, opened her legs, bit the back of her neck
and did to her what any Englishman should do to his wife,
(though it's more Christian and seemly, so our Priest tells us,
to lie her flat on her back) and I must say the sight
of her white shoulders and the twin hillocks of her arse
fired up my blood as though I was seventeen again –
but what a hollering and bellowing fuss she made, as though
I was some vagabond who'd shoved her up against the wall
in a tavern passage to ruin her reputation, not her lawful
husband who'd fed and kept her even though she'd never
given me a child in five years of wedlock – I paid no heed
to all her noise, I knew what was right, and when I was spent
she leapt off the bed, sobbing and shouting and calling me
names the Devil himself would use, she squared her shoulders,
boxed me full in the face with both fists, one-two, one-two.

*   *   *

And after that, I swear to God I tried to resist but what's a man
to do when he finds just a glimpse of bosom turns his thoughts
to sin and soon I was sniffing round every wench in the village,
and sometimes I got an afternoon of pleasure in a hayloft – or
a few angry fathers and husbands threatening to cut off my
manhood and nail it to the church door, but some fierce need
in me kept rising, some force where the urge to rut like a beast
was stronger than fear of God or man or my wife – and thirty seven
days after *that* night, there *she* was, lips so tightly pressed
they might have been stitched, her belly a rolling barrel and
such frenzy under the skin, such punching, jumping and
wriggling, and then she ups and wraps up a bundle of blankets
and such and off she lumbers into the field, larks screaming
high overhead and when I found her that evening, curled

31

up and dreamy-tired, what do I discover but that I'm a father,
and it's four she's had, all sticky and bloody and mewling,
two of them clamped to her nipples and the Lord preserve us,
there she is licking one, tonguing its wet brown fur because
it's more animal than human, an abomination and I cry out
What Devil's work is this, woman? and, as God is my witness,
she looks up, peels her lips apart and bares her wicked teeth.

Vegetarian Hangover

Mornings like these; the true test of commitment. A rat's died in my mouth, an orchestra's tuning up in my head and I give in; I need a bacon sandwich. Unsmoked, Danish, a little ketchup. I peel three rashers, pale fat sliming the cellophane, listen to the hiss as I drop them into hot oil, edges curling – that pink, browning. I salivate, press them between slices of Kingsmill Thick Cut – bite into the centre, fingers and chin luminous. Last night's antics seem amusing – heroic, even – in a way they never are over mueseli and peppermint tea.

And I won't think of the farm holiday when I was taken to see a butcher grip a pig between his knees, won't remember its squeal just before the gun shot, the man whistling as he slit its throat – the spurt of blood into a bucket, his striped apron spattered crimson and the long, dark coil of guts. I'll think instead of Cockaigne, where happy pigs trotted round with knives in their backs waiting to be carved, eager to feed anyone who'd drunk too deeply of life's pleasures; no conscience troubled, no guilt due – no nightmares of blood-stained concrete or a smiling butcher, and his long knife.

The Spaghetti Harvest

On 1ˢᵗ April 1957, BBC's 'Panorama' announced that due to a very mild winter and the virtual elimination of the dreaded spaghetti weevil, Swiss farmers were enjoying a bumper crop. Huge numbers of viewers called the BBC asking how they could grow their own spaghetti tree.

Not for us, the back-breaking digging,
Wellingtons sinking deep into sticky mud,

spade-handles callusing our hands.
No, we've switched, gone Continental.

We started with one tree, but now we've
a small orchard! At harvest time,

the whole family's involved. Up at dawn
for prayers round the table, giving thanks

for God's great blessing – the mild winter,
early spring. We sing the special

harvesting song as we reach up, pluck
damp strands for our wicker baskets.

It's a marvel, how straight
and blonde it is. *Like a Princess's hair!*

our daughters say. You can't say that
about spuds, can you? We lay it

on towels, dry it in the sun. It keeps
for months, never loses flavour.

Our neighbours no longer speak to us,
leave their windows open

when they're roasting potatoes
in duck-fat and home-grown rosemary.

Gourmets

Three of us in a Malaga bar, the scent of lemons inviting itself through open windows. After plump oiled olives and salty Calamari, my friends agree – Jamon Iberico is the finest cured ham, from black Iberian acorn-fed pigs; a delicacy, a rare treat. They take up their forks; the meat on the white plate translucent as holy wafers, red as ox-blood Doc Martens. He eats a whole slice quickly, closes his eyes. *Rich in oleic acid,* he says, *very good for lowering cholesterol.* He believes that to eat every scrap and leave no trace is to honour the animal, the sacrifice it's made; but she leaves pale, creamy strips piled on the side of her plate. She's only after the meat; the pig died anyway, it's past taking offence. They bicker about the acorns; he says he's enjoying the delicate nutty undertone; she says, *Bullshit, humans can't detect the taste.* He laughs, cleans his plate with his bread and they lay their forks side by side, wipe grease from fingers, sated now. With Manzanilla sherry, light and dry as a warm wind, they toast the butcher who scrubbed his hands, secured the leg in the holder, chopped off the hoof, slivered off yellow rind, sliced round bone, through muscle. And to the pig, who rooted, grunting, for the pale acorns, its ears flapping over its eyes.

Apples

She ate an apple
and swallowed a pip.

Her brother said
You'll grow a tree inside.

At first she was scared;
felt the pip burrow,

sink and take hold.
New roots quivered,

fattened and spread;
the trunk thickened,

split into branches.
Then leaves itched free,

fluttered inside her.
When the blossom burst,

her belly swelled,
a new landscape.

She ran through rain
with her face to the sky

thanking God, and full
of her own apples.

The Set of Optics You Wouldn't Let Me Buy in Portobello Market, September 1984

Remember how I fell in love with them,
how they glinted in the weak sunlight
among the tarnished soup tureens,
scratched fob-watches? My hand reached out
to trace the inscriptions – *whisky, gin, vermouth.*
Oh that word, vermouth –
evenings in a silk kimono, louche, bohemian,
sipping a way of life. Rachmaninov.
I'd have fixed them above my desk
in my high-ceilinged study
with its polished floors, I'd sit on
a green and gold Lloyd Loom chair,
overlooking a lush jungle of a garden.
That glug of spirits – *ah, ah, ah* ....
My own private bar. Look, if I'd bought them
I'd have stayed out of sleazy pubs
and drifted round my Hampstead flat,
thin and mysterious; I'd have written
that trilogy of exquisite novels, I'd be
taking a call from my agent –
the film rights – *Megabucks,*
darling, and when can we do lunch?
Remember how I fell in love with them?
My hand reached out. Oh, that word. Vermouth.

Merlot

Furious with her ex-lover, she opens
a decent bottle of Merlot,
fills a glass almost to the top
and within minutes
he's up to his knees
in a dark red lake
wind-milling his arms.
She drinks steadily until
he's waist deep, flailing.
He shouts up – *Remember*
sunrise on Westminster Bridge,
my hands on your breasts?
The flat in Kennington –
you bit my thumb to the bone?
She pours another glass.
Once he's fully submerged,
she sighs, closes her eyes –
finally appreciating the Merlot's
musty fruit; its full, robust body.

The Mushroom Season

*After a domestic burglary, it was discovered that the radio
had been tuned to Radio Four.*
         – Guardian, 2000

In the master bedroom, Roy re-tunes
to *You and Yours*. This Peter White –
poor chap's blind, but cultured, clever,
voice warm as a scarf, or winter soup.

It's the mushroom season, says Peter,
and foragers are out in force. Roy eases
open the bottom drawer, removes both
passports, an envelope of pristine Euros,

holds a green necklace up to the light.
Emeralds, delicate, very nicely set.
Now Peter's talking to a mushroom expert chap,
a *mycologist,* he started picking at eight –

his grandparents' farm during the war –
half a crown a pound. Small fortune
in those days. *Enterprising,* thinks Roy,
wrapping the necklace in tissue,

remembering the dank, sunless woods
behind the Fairview estate, clusters of pale,
fleshy mushrooms, shy under trees;
how, when you snapped one in half,

the insides were ridged, like gills – you
almost thought they'd pulse – and daring
his mate – *Eat one!* The mushroom people
are off to the New Forest now – all echoey,

squelchy sounds – and they meet another
forager, with his bag, his soil-stained fingers.

It's become my passion, for my own pleasure,
my own consumption. Roy nods at that,

heads next door to the study, where a skinny
Mac Book perches on a beech desk; bags it
carefully, and now from the bedroom there's
another voice, warning – poisonous ones;

Death Cap, Destroying Angel, Deadly Web Cap,
Fool's Web Cap and False Morel – you'd have
fatal kidney damage – some are rusty brown,
easily mistaken for Chanterelles. Nasty.

The voice says, *An abundance of caution*
is a useful tool. Roy thinks *Too right,*
bubble-wraps an I-Pod, a Sony camera.
Now back to the mycologist, the main man –

Black Trumpet, he says, *they call them*
Trumpet de Mort in French, super to eat.
Roy zips the bag; nearly lunch-time.
Black Trumpet, he thinks, *beautiful name.*

Much more to this mycology lark than
he'd realised. One day, he'll go foraging
himself, he'll study the science of it, do it
properly; after all they're free, mushrooms,

nature's bounty; there for the taking,
so long as you're careful, so long as you
follow the rules. He pads down the thickly
carpeted stairs, the radio still talking to itself;

clicks the back door shut, peels off his gloves,
thinks of woods full of scuffling bracken –
bird-song, damp earth, and mushrooms –
delicious, innocent – waiting to be pulled.

Spring Equinox

Tonight the clocks
move forward
and we'll lose an hour.
What happens to it?
I ask the taxi driver.
Where does it go, exactly?

He raises the volume
on his Chinese language tape.
Voices trill through the car;
questions; responses.

It sounds like singing.

And then the car fills
– jasmine blossom,
spiced pork;
bicycle bells,
wind charms.

A woman kneels
in the sodden foot-well
to harvest rice.

This is the future,
he tells me,
communication.
You have to be
one step ahead.

They'll be running the world
soon enough.

He puts his foot down
and we zoom
up the high street,
it's nearly midnight,
then it's tomorrow,
and then. And then.

The Pianos

On the last day, when the sky turns red,
the piano in Brighton's Grand hotel
will start to perform the *Moonlight Sonata*.

The gleaming black and ivory notes
will ripple up and down, like a breeze

shivering over a cornfield. As the floor
churns, the piano will tip and tilt but play on,
pianissimo, hardly audible beneath

the crashing masonry, shattering glass;
within minutes every single piano

on the South Coast will join in,
and the summons will spread inland,
east, west and north, to Scotland,

Wales and Ireland, and then to Europe,
America, Africa, India, Antartica ...

piano shall call to piano.
By the stormy final movement,
they'll relish the difficult chromasticism,

the arpeggios, they will make music
for each other, for the final ferocity.

They will not go meekly, the pianos,
they will play until the earth splits open,
roars them down for the Underworld gods.

Please Select a Product

One a.m. Sleet. Yellow light from the *Photo-Me* booth pools on the station's platform. Blue curtain drawn back. Black screen. Fingerprints. A woman's voice. Haughty. *Please select a product.* The station manager locks the gates, drives home. Two rats patter along humming rails. Glittering eyes. Naked tails. *Please select a product.* The rats sniff a damp paper bag. Scramble inside. Crusts. Tomato slices. The bag vibrates. *When you have made your selection, please insert the correct money. When you have made your selection ...* One rat backs out. First snowflakes tremble on its fur as it runs. *Please select a product ...* The bag. Thumping.

The Sanctification of Clacket Lane Services, Westbound

It's done overnight, without fuss
– a Midnight blessing, holy water sprinkled
onto formica and pine, in dim light.
So, by morning, Costa's cappuccinos
have become the blood of Christ
for slumped Sales Managers
who stare at the car-park wondering
how their waistlines disappeared under
a soft mulch of fat, why their wives
no longer kiss them fully on the lips.
Now it's a new Cathedral
for transient congregations, floods
of hungry, whey-faced souls washed up
into its halls, its echoing corridors –
teenagers texted by the Holy Spirit,
games machines suddenly luminous
with the Annunciation, Gabriel's hand
on Mary's shoulder. The dark recesses
of the Gents are places of confession,
men mouthing silently, their brows
unclenched. The blessing of a particular tap
in the Ladies' means hot water flowing
over a woman's hands leaves her
with a sense of purity, peace,
her palms free of the taint of money
she'd used to pacify the kids –
for burgers, fries, and mega-cokes
black as Priests' robes. And when
those customers leave, redeemed,
the drone and burr of traffic will soothe
like Plainsong, or a call to prayer.

Namesake

*Catherine of Siena (1347-1380), a Scholastic philosopher
and theologian, was thought to suffer from Anorexia
Mirabilis; starving in the name of God, sustained by
ascetic ecstacy and the pus and scabs of lepers.*

Catherine, twenty-third child of a cloth dyer
and a poet's daughter – your twin sister

languishing on the wet nurse's nipple,
half your siblings already dead. At five,

your holy visions threw you to your knees
in pious ecstasy. Febrile convulsions –

juddering teeth, puppet limbs – left me
with a bleeding tongue, in wet knickers.

I'm my parents' only daughter, truculent,
kicked out of Baptist Sunday School

at eleven for arguing with Mrs Wilson
about the Virgin Birth. You survived

the Black Death, searing heat, open sewers.
I outlived the threat of Cold War, Cuban

Missile crisis; small-town boredom.

        ❋   ❋   ❋

Our name means 'pure.' Hunger's pure,
denial at its purest. There I was –

grapefruit segments, cottage cheese;
there you were, claiming you never felt

hunger, or if you did, nibbling a leper's
pus-filled scabs. Did you used to curl up

with blinding headaches, Catherine,
did your skin ever itch and flake,

did your guts growl when you lay,
praying for perfection? Did you once faint,

smash your eyebrow on a tiled floor?
You starved for God, your jutting ribcage

holy. I did it to disappear, to float above
my life. You talked with Jesus in your head.

Was he nice? I hope so. In *my* head,
a skinny dancer in pink Lycra whispered

Pig whenever I opened the fridge.

*   *   *

Neither of us fazed by blood. Moments
before a young man was beheaded,

you knelt, made the sign of the cross,
whispered of the blood of the lamb

as his lips murmured *Jesus and Catherine*
and he was still murmuring when

his head slipped into your hands,
and you caught and cradled it,

his blood scenting your cloak and skin.
You couldn't bear to scrub it off.

And once, in a pub, a young man
with a smashed-up face allowed me

to bathe his wounds with soaking
paper towels from the Ladies', as

he bled all over my hands, my new
purple dress. *I'm sorry,* he said,

through swollen lips, *What's your name,
by the way?* And when I told him,

he nodded. *A Saint's name. Saint's name.*

The Lip Stitcher

I come with my little bag
            – needles and gauze,
cat-gut and scissors.

Every lip's
            a cushion, a jelly-fish
full of nerve-endings.
                        Every stab is agony.
Blood pools,
            blackens like warm tar.

I have stitched the lips
            of lovers who fear they'll
cry out in their sleep;
            the lips of asylum seekers
in flithy, blistering
            detention camps
and on the steps of cold
            stone Altars
in English churches.

I have stitched the lips
            of Bolivian prostitutes
who swore they'd starve
            if the brothels closed,
if they couldn't fill
            their mouths with
their regulars' cocks.

I have stitched the lips
            of blasphemers and Saints
and those who crave
            the pain of the needle –
who winced
            but wanted more
in basements
            in Hackney
and Birmingham.

I have stitched the lips
            of the dead,
so the soul stays put,
            and won't cry out.

I come with my little bag
            – needles and gauze,
cat-gut and scissors.

Mary's Ear Explains The Immaculate Conception

An early Christian notion held that Christ was conceived by the Holy Ghost entering the Virgin Mary's ear; hence the dove at Mary's ear in some annunciation scenes.

Everyone wonders how it was done –
the passing of God's seed to a simple girl
who'd never opened her legs. Listen;

the dove parted the curtain of her hair
with his white head, slipped inside me,
his throat bulging. I felt the jab

and jut of his closed beak, I was full,
full of his cooing, the roar and echo of it,
then the judder of release – sudden heat,

flooding. I was full and then empty,
sticky and drained and as he backed out
the curtain of her hair swung closed, left me

in darkness. This is the truth of it. I was
the organ, the chamber, the tunnel
entrance. In the beginning, it started here.

Beginning Her Sentence at Holloway

When they ask her where she's from
she says, *Paradise, but I got chucked out.*

I'm the original bad girl, it's all down to me.
That bastard creature wormed his way

into my heart, my head, my mouth.
I'm the fool who crunched the apple's flesh

and let the juices dribble down my chin
like spunk. Sisters, I was up to no good

before you lot were even thought of!
The women share their tobacco with her,

she's clearly in her own league.
So, asks a blonde who'd stabbed

her husband after a night on cheap cider,
What was that Adam like, then? And God?

She draws hard on her roll-up, rolls her eyes;
Oh, Adam was a total prick. Nag, nag, nag.

God was just cross and distant. I reckon
he hated women. Anyway, she says,

I was young and stupid; you try living
on grapes and figs and rules.

The officers keep their eyes on her. She's
trouble, this one, a loud-mouthed fantasist.

And that afternoon the staff ignore the noises;
five women burst into her cell, hold her down,

strip and pelt her with used tampons –
That'll teach you, bitch! They don't call it

the curse for nothing! Three days out of thirty
I'm off my head, spat a mother of five,

and as for childbirth, fuck that! If you'd learned
to keep your eyes down and your gob shut

none of this would have happened!
She's found next morning, naked,

small and shrivelled as discarded peel,
the smell of apples souring in her hair.

Attending Adam's Funeral

Such a hot, sultry day, the air
weighted with rose-scent, birds
singing their throats out.

She stares into the fresh hole,
its sliced and scarred soil,
as the men lower ropes
and his coffin settles. *Man*
that is born of woman has but
a short time to live, mumbles
the Priest. *Man that was*
God's favourite creature lived long.
Adam, Adam. Your wounded
side. The wrenched-out bone.

Mourners dab their eyes;
clods of earth thud the lid.

Cain stifles a yawn, Abel swigs
single malt from a hip-flask and she
kneels, drops an apple core

onto the dead centre of the wood.

Retirement, The Paradise View Rest Home

Summer mornings, alone, she wanders the garden,
grass moist and lush under orthopaedic shoes,

stoops to tickle the cat's velvet head,
checks flower-beds for adders, scoops them

tenderly, feeling their warm bellies pulse
in her palm, then drowns them in the water butt.

The T.V. room reeks – hyacinths and piss –
but the staff are kind, don't mention her sons,

encourage her to join in Communal Singing,
Music and Movement. *Mustn't let the joints seize up,*

says Mrs. Clark. *Keep the mind active. The bible,
if you must, but not the gloomy bits. Crosswords!*

She's made so many friends. Salome's next door,
lends her racy thrillers; Jezebel, Delilah, Lott's wife

and several ladies from Sodom and Gomorrah bring
windfalls for her secret cider press. She hosts

soirées on Sunday nights; serious drinkers only.
The Whore of Babylon brings peanuts, olives, figs.

Otherwhere

in the minutes before
       it began –

           before it knocked you over
           rolled your eyes up into your head –

– we'd sat in the café drinking
tea eating toast talking about days
when everything seemed out of
control as though nothing we said
or did made sense like a joke
the gods played on us when they
grew bored of shape-shifting
or rape or eating their children
and just as we finally agreed
yes that's probably it you

      stood up and walked back forth back forth

         and I said   *what are you doing can I help you*
                        can I help you what do you need

you bit through your tongue
         the raw meat of your tongue
            slashed open all pink inside
and I said
oh you poor sweetheart
                blood on your lips and
teeth

you weren't there any more
you were
other
where

where are you
you were

electricity

and you said *call an ambulance please call*
where is it where the fuck is it
I need it now where is it call again

and even when you sat down
calm calm no longer shaking *good girl good girl*
you'd already left
you'd been taken
come back come back

*   *   *   *   *

you lay in the ambulance
bruised and still

you're fine now fine now
everything's fine you're fine now

– the gods had had their fun with you –

pissing themselves laughing you
cruel bastards stay where you are
leave her alone now leave her alone

Story

She went to the shop and she bought
a wedding dress. She went to the shop

and she bought a wedding dress and
a husband. She went to the shop

and she bought a wedding dress,
a husband and a baby. Then the husband

buttoned her into the wedding dress
and cut it open at the front so

she could put the baby to the breast
and he sucked, sucked and sucked

all day and half the night
and the husband went out for hours

to the woods to trap weasels and rabbits
for meat, and skins to wrap the baby in

and the walls pressed in and in until
she could hardly breathe and then one day

she walked out to the woods and found
a clearing and took off the dress and

felt the cool air on her skin and it
felt good. And she made a hammock

of the dress between two old oaks
and in time grew a pelt to keep her

warm and learned to trap weasels
and rabbits and roast them on her fire

and at night she lay in her hammock-dress.
She looked up at the sky and mapped the stars.

*   *   *

She went to the woods and mapped the dress
and roasted the stars. She went

to the woods and mapped the dress, roasted
the stars and grew weasels and rabbits.

She went to the woods and mapped the dress,
roasted the stars, grew weasels and rabbits

and made a hammock of the husband.
She walked to a clearing and took off

the husband. She walked to a clearing
and took off the husband and the baby.

She walked to a clearing and there was no shop.
She lay in the sky and mapped the dress.

Nectar

The hottest day so far. A bee
mutters by the open window.
Andy asks who'd like to start.

Ken says his dad used a hammer,
shows us the scar on his scalp.
Morag says that's no excuse

for self-pity, she's had far worse
and anyway scars heal, but
the voices in her head won't shut up,

she needs to go home, tidy the larder,
re-arrange all the tins and jars – size,
content, shade, texture, date.

Peter says she should do what he's done,
ask the Lord to cast out demons,
fill her brim-full with the Spirit.

Andy chews a finger-nail. The bee
scrapes its back legs and watches,
waiting for me to rise from my chair,

wrap my legs around its belly, plunge
to the nearest rose-bed. Andy asks
if there's anything I'd like to say.

I'd like to say *drink* and *nectar*
but the words swell in my throat,
the bee vibrates and zooms away.

Time's up; we drift into the garden
and tilt our faces to the sun.
Beyond the wall there's a hive; honey.

She Sits Like a Bird

The battle is over
                The mother has won
Norman is no longer
                You have to go back
The battle is over
                Ten years it's been over
Norman is no longer
                She met a new man
The battle is over
                You have to go back
Norman is no longer
                She threw him over
The battle is over
                His mother took over
He stole her corpse
                He weighted her coffin
The battle is over
                He wore her clothes
He wore her hair
                She wore him down
She threw him over
                The mother was jealous
The battle is over
                Like a dutiful son
He wore her hair
                When reality took over
He was never all Norman
                He began to speak for her
Hid her in the fruit cellar
                She threw him over
He dressed in her clothes
                He had to speak for her

The battle is over
        She sat in the cellar
He weighted her coffin
        The mother has won
She asks for a blanket
        The battle is over
It's sad when a mother
        Norman is over
Has to speak the words
        He wore her hair
That condemn her own son
        The battle is over
She feels a little chill
        He stuffed the birds
She sits very quiet
        She won't harm a fly
She won't harm her boy
        She sits like a bird
Its innards all padded
        She won't harm a fly
The battle is over
        Norman is over
She sits very quiet
        She won't harm a fly

The Lump

The morning after
his father's funeral,

a man wakes
with a lump

in his throat
so solid he can

hardly breathe.
His Doctor says,

*You've swallowed
your father, I'm afraid,*

*and he's sticking
in your throat.*

*It's essential you
cut him out at once.*

He gives the man
a scalpel, mirror, bowl,

towel, needle, thread.
The man's hands

shake but he slices
open his own flesh

and the lump is
indeed his father,

crumpled, blood-soaked;
he scoops the little

man out, places him
in the bowl and

covers it with the towel.
He stitches his throat,

slow and calm;
promises himself

a cold beer,
a dish of oysters.

Afterpains

Nobody tells you this – that when
your second baby latches on the nipple,
the womb, lonely and vicious,
clenches itself, again and again,
fists and thumps, or snarls
into a cat's cradle,
makes you want to push
your child away, this innocent
torturer clamped and hungry;
nobody says, the price you pay
for doing things by the book,
for offering your breasts like holy gifts
is a body furious with you,
a womb still sullenly contracting,
nobody tells you this tightening
is the womb's last gasp,
because the sadness of it
might linger, might cause you to
grieve, leak useless tears
onto your newborn's scalp,
and you might not understand
or forgive. And you must forgive.

Anywhere

For days her body's birthed
clots of black blood.

This afternoon, three hours
of the baby's wailing.

Can't silence him with
her breasts, her rocking.

Stands in the wet garden,
thinking of fast trains.

London. Glasgow. Anywhere.

Back at the Aunt's House You Haven't

A bored, distracted child?
her skirt's loose thread, like
here, and why do her hands pull at
remember your name or why you're
a small, quiet voice, why doesn't she
and why does the aunt speak in such
beans struggling to cling to canes,
cabbages frilled and rotting, green
is the lawn so bald and patchy,
belly-surf down, arms flailing – why
a park, that grassy slope you could
and the garden – you'd thought it was
the dark red circles are barely there
the rug you'd land on, faded so much
no longer high enough to jump off
through – the living room chairs –
enough to stick head and shoulders
the serving hatch only just big
coloured iron, cold to the touch –
the colossal Aga's a lump of toffee
remembered as ballroom-long; now
cross the yellow kitchen you
good strides from door to window
have shrunk – you could take four
visited for thirty-five years, the rooms
Back at the aunt's house you haven't

Colours

The summer you were ten, celandines
        rampaged through flowerbeds. Stains
on the gardener's hands where he'd
        pulled them up by the roots. His palm

across your mouth.

        Today in the supermarket, you saw all those
little suns trapped in the big freezers.

        It made you cry and people stared.

A man with a green badge was kind.

        But then, the ambulance, with its
weeping, the gash of yellow along
its side; you couldn't stop shaking.

        The psychiatrist had fat purple veins
in his hands and neck, and a red pen,
        a black notebook with blue lines.

He asked about the celandines – they always
        do – but you know he wanted to whisper,
        What colour knickers are you
        wearing? You have to be on your
guard in these places. Any moment,
some bastard could pin you down,

        hold a buttercup under your chin.

Thrift

In the changing room you tell yourself
this need to wear what others discard

is all about recycling, thrift – then slip
another woman's black silk evening dress

over your head, feed your arms through
the fluted sleeves, as she must have done –

watched by her husband as he sat
on the marital bed, or by her lover,

in a hotel room, after sex and before
dinner. Under the naked light-bulb,

you ease the zip from hip to arm-pit;
become the shapely Goddess she must

have been, waist miraculously cinched,
breasts pillowing over the neckline.

The dress remembers her perfume –
musky, expensive – and her sweat, her

pheromones imprinted for the men
who breathed her in, wanted her,

wanted her so badly each one knelt
at her feet. This other woman's

dress sharpens your cheekbones,
brightens your eyes; maybe it will

gift you a love of opera; fluent Italian.
You leave with it scrolled in your bag, with

her husband at your elbow, her lover
close behind, pining for one last touch.

After a Saturday Teaching Nine-Year-Olds to Write Poetry
For Brendan Cleary

Essential that *Seagull's Breakfast*
breezes over the finishing line
first in the 3.15 at Punchestown
in order that your visit to the bookies
will be all smiles and bonhomie.
And your lover's lips must be soft
as you splash a young Spanish rioja
into heavy tumblers, and the light
through the window should linger
a moment on the curve of her cheek;
and tonight's Spaghetti Bolognese
you'll cook, together, between kisses,
will be a triumph – the sauce meaty
and rich, the pasta *al dente*.
Next you must walk with your lover
to the public bar of *The Bear* –
soothed by the scent of Harveys Old Mild
you'll find a room full of mates
full of Arsenal's triumph, and later,
as you and she sway home
through the freezing air, you'll gaze
at Orion blazing over the racecourse
and her tongue must yield to yours
as easily as a cat slips its paw
into butter ... and please God,
let sleep arrive easily tonight,
a seamless slippage into that dream
where the six horse accumulator
finally comes good –
the glorious cacophony of hooves
streaming past, so close you can see
the Venetian blinds of muscles
moving in their cheeks –
all the pounding and the dust,
at last, all home, all safe home.

Intimacy

Rush-hour, Central line. Tube doors
shush together, I'm squashed against
this unknown woman, we're almost
skin to skin. I keep my eyes down but
I've already clocked every minute line
feathering her mouth, the splash of blue
on one brown pupil, black stitching
around the popper inside her coat;
a loose thread on her magenta
jumper's sleeve; the gilt of her ear-rings;
hint of Cardamom on her breath.
At this moment I know her better
than her colleagues, her mother,
her husband, her lover. I could lean
forward and taste her flushed cheek.
If she dropped dead, now, and I
was called upon to describe her
last moments I'd say, she was sick
of all this travelling, rushing from
place to place and going nowhere,
she wanted something better;
solitude and silence perhaps. I'd say
she needed to feel the wind in her hair;
that a tiny muscle twitched
and jumped under her left eye.

Zephyr

As I return to my sensible Passat
in Tesco's car park, I still
expect to see the Zephyr, brooding –
that fuck-off hulk of a motor
you bought for three hundred quid
from a Birmingham art student, 1979;
two tons of scratched black metal,
lacquered red and orange flames
licking the doors and fenders.
I remember the M1 muffled with
blinding snow, Led Zeppelin, full blast;
fingers freezing inside my gloves,
lighting your Marlboroughs,
handing them over as you squinted
into the low sun. I loved your dark hair
curling into the nape of your neck,
your white, even teeth. And always,
always, your hand pressed on my knee
would dry my mouth, part my legs –
you'd find a slip-road, park in a clearing
and unravel me from my layers,
thumbing my jeans to my knees.
You kept your scratchy sweater on,
the one that flamed my nipples.
The leatherette bench seat where we slid
– our breath, fogging the blue air, while
the engine tutted and you – you,
pressing me down, exploding
inside me like a meteor shower.
Ah, the sex, the raw, tricky sex
we had in that car – I remember too
the times it flounced to a standstill
or refused to start after a bellyful of fuel –

you'd sit tight, I'd be sent to recruit
nonplussed lorry drivers to help push
the bastard off forecourts.
That night in hushed Moseley where
it sputtered messily up a side-street,
coughed and died, on our way to a party –
and I'm wide-eyed, Southern-posh,
can in hand, *Could we have*
some water, please, for the car,
yes, sorry, we're students, sorry –
to a startled, aproned woman
halfway through peeling spuds.
And if I saw it now, would I have the guts
to snap the locks, hot-wire it,
listen to the engine gurgle, ease
its bulk towards the exit, my foot
fluttering the brake as your fingers
once fluttered inside me? Rummage
through the glove compartment
for your stash of Wriggley's Freshmint,
or one final, desiccated cigarette,
mutter, *Come on, you useless pile of crap,*
you freak, you ghost – eighteen again,
rotten with desire – would I laugh
as the beast jerked into life, could I
grip the wheel, peer into low sun,
jam my foot down, and head north?

The White Sheets

How wicked this feels, to sneak back
to our room mid-morning, windows open,
curtains drawn against the sun.

We undress each other silently,
skin still warm from the street
where minutes ago we breathed in

slow-cooking lamb. Your mouth
tastes of melon, chorizo,
salami, dolcelatte, espresso –

and as you slide a pillow
under my buttocks, the white sheets
cool against my shoulders, I open

like the petals of a lotus. I don't
cry out, half expecting the manager
to rap on the door, point out

we're contravening some regulation
in the small print. We shouldn't
be inside, we should be exploring

the hushed cool of a back-street chapel,
breathing in the Mother of God,
lighting candles for our dead. Instead

we fuck with the urgency of new lovers
in a dingy King's Cross hotel,
aware afterwards of the dull throb of traffic,

the scratches on each other's backs.

Prayers

Because you promised
to process his application for
the caretaker's position
as quickly as possible,
he's including you,
nightly, in his prayers.

He rings next morning,
to check; you assure him
the paperwork's in order.
He tells you he'll include
your parents and brothers
in his prayers.

That night you imagine him
kneeling on the floor
in a bed-sit in Hounslow,
the sour orange glow
from a streetlight
seeking out his tight hands.

When he rings you
two days later, he sounds tired.
His prayers, he tells you,
take him a long time.

There's his own family
to consider – his wife
who longs to join him,
his brother whose feet
still suppurate from
after the arrest,
the beatings. His country,

he tells you, is a place
where bad men come
in the night. And

the nightmares, still.
From now on, he'll be including
your aunts, cousins,
surviving grandfather,
friends, in his prayers.

Next morning you wake
in a room flooded with sunlight,
drink hot tea and hope
his lips aren't cracked –

and when he rings
he apologizes for bothering you,
but tells you again
how much this job
would mean.

This job. You are
a kind English lady,
and tonight in his prayers
he'll include, lady,
your future husband,
and your future babies,
if you are so blessed.

Stalled

The snow's pristine, glittering
on both banks of the M25;
a snowman, plump and perky
in his Arsenal hat and scarf,
beams from the central reservation.
The Labrador sitting in the Volvo
in front mists the rear window
with his patient breath.
My heater meditates on a low,
steady hum. I close my eyes.
I'm going nowhere. There's just
this mint sucked to sugar
on my tongue, Satie's *Gymnopedies*
tingling through the speakers.
I take my hands from the wheel;
can't imagine moving now,
the world blurring past.
Every breath since my birth
has led here and all there is
is this stalled moment –
how can I say it is not perfect?

Smith/Doorstop Books, Pamphlets and Audio

25 years
of titles by

Moniza Alvi, Simon Armitage, Jane Aspinall, Ann Atkinson, Annemarie Austin, Sally Baker, Mike Barlow, Kate Bass, Suzanne Batty, Chris Beckett, Peter Bennet, Catherine Benson, Gerard Benson, Sujata Bhatt, Nina Boyd, Sue Boyle, Susan Bright, Carole Bromley, Sue Butler, Liz Cashdan, Dennis Casling, Julia Casterton, Clare Chapman, Linda Chase, Debjani Chatterjee, Chris Considine, Stanley Cook, Bob Cooper, Jennifer Copley, Paula Cunningham, Simon Currie, Duncan Curry, Ann Dancy, Peter Daniels, Jonathan Davidson, Kwame Dawes, Julia Deakin, Steve Dearden, Patricia Debney, Mike Di Placido, Tim Dooley, Jane Draycott, Carol Ann Duffy, Sue Dymoke, Nell Farrell, Catherine Fisher, Janet Fisher, Sam Gardiner, Adele Geras, Sally Goldsmith, Yvonne Green, Harry Guest, Robert Hamberger, Sophie Hannah, John Harvey, Jo Haslam, Geoff Hattersley, Jeanette Hattersley, Marko Hautala, Selima Hill, Andrea Holland, Sian Hughes, Keith Jafrate, Lesley Jeffries, Chris Jones, Mimi Khalvati, John Killick, Stephen Knight, Judith Lal, John Lancaster, Peter Lane, Michael Laskey, Brenda Lealman, Tim Liardet, John Lyons, Cheryl Martin, Eleanor Maxted, John McAuliffe, Michael McCarthy, Patrick McGuinness, Kath Mckay, Paul McLoughlin, Hugh McMillan, Ian McMillan, Allison McVety, Hilary Menos, Paul Mills, Hubert Moore, David Morley, Paul Munden, Les Murray, Dorothy Nimmo, Stephanie Norgate, Christopher North, Carita Nystrom, Sean O'Brien, Padraig O'Morain, Alan Payne, Pascale Petit, Ann Pilling, Jim Pollard, Simon Rae, Irene Rawnsley, Ed Reiss, Padraig Rooney, Jane Routh, Michael Schmidt, Myra Schneider, Ted Schofield, Kathryn Simmonds, Lemn Sissay, Felicity Skelton, Catherine Smith, Elspeth Smith, Joan Jobe Smith, Cherry Smyth, Pauline Stainer, Martin Stannard, Adam Strickson, Mandy Sutter, Diana Syder, Pam Thompson, Susan Utting, Steven Waling, Martyn Wiley, Andrew Wilson, River Wolton, Sue Wood, Anna Woodford, Mary Woodward, Cliff Yates …

www.poetrybusiness.co.uk

Lightning Source UK Ltd.
Milton Keynes UK
UKOW032317081012

200263UK00001B/15/P